# Harmonic Echoes

## Also by Trixi Field

*Your Song Your Joy*
*Jazzicle Pops!*

# Harmonic Echoes

*Ten simple canonic chants
for choirs, small groups of singers
voice workshops and schools*

## Trixi Field

**MP3 downloads of backings and sample
performances are available by visiting:
www.lulu.com/trixifield**

Third Edition
Voice Confidence
*www.trixifield.co.uk*

# Harmonic Echoes

## Trixi Field

Published by
Voice Confidence
Hemel Hempstead
United Kingdom
voice.confidence@gmail.com
www.trixifield.co.uk

All rights reserved. No part of this publication may be reproduced or transmitted in any form or by any means, digital, electronic or mechanical, including photocopying or recording or by any information storage and retrieval system without permission from the author, except for the inclusion of brief quotations in a review.

Original copyright © 2007 Trixi Field
Second edition © 2008 Trixi Field
Third edition © 2009 Trixi Field

Cover photograph "Rocks at Dawn" © 2005 Trixi Field
Back cover image "Echo of the Rocks" © 2009 Trixi Field
Portrait of the author © 2008 Daniela Walter

ISBN: 978-0-9559805-2-7

# Contents

|     |                                      | Page |
| --- | ------------------------------------ | ---- |
|     | Introduction                         | 1    |
| 1.  | Sing a Song of Life                  | 3    |
|     | Notes                                | 4    |
|     | Music                                | 5    |
| 2.  | Be Peace                             | 7    |
|     | Notes                                | 8    |
|     | Music                                | 9    |
| 3.  | Dusk Chant                           | 11   |
|     | Notes                                | 12   |
|     | Music                                | 13   |
| 4.  | Peace, Sweet and Gentle              | 15   |
|     | Notes                                | 16   |
|     | Music                                | 17   |
| 5.  | My Heart Be Still                    | 19   |
|     | Notes                                | 20   |
|     | Music                                | 21   |
| 6.  | Still Voices                         | 23   |
|     | Notes                                | 24   |
|     | Music                                | 25   |
| 7.  | Dawn Chant                           | 27   |
|     | Notes                                | 28   |
|     | Music                                | 29   |
| 8.  | We Are The Song                      | 31   |
|     | Notes                                | 32   |
|     | Music                                | 33   |
| 9.  | Adorian (Peace Be In Our Hearts)     | 35   |
|     | Notes                                | 36   |
|     | Music                                | 37   |
| 10. | Light, Soft and Gentle               | 39   |
|     | Notes                                | 40   |
|     | Music                                | 41   |
|     | Lyrics                               | 43   |
|     | About the author                     | 55   |

# *Introduction*

The Canon is a most interesting musical structure. Its simplest and most accessible form is generally known as a 'round' or a 'catch' – a melodic line sung first by one voice or group of voices, and then imitated, note for note, by more voices or groups of voices every few bars (measures), creating a harmonic and melodic echo effect.

Perhaps the best known examples of this kind of canon are: "Three Blind Mice", "London's Burning", "Frère Jacques" and "Row, Row, Row Your Boat".

Canons have an interesting effect on the listener. The involvement of all the voices together gives, on the one hand, a feeling of motionlessness, since all parts of the melodic line are sung simultaneously for as long as all the voices are involved. The canon doesn't seem to be going anywhere.

Yet, at the same time, since each voice or group of voices is at a different point in the canon, the melody seems to swish around the singers in a kind of aural "Mexican wave".

Whilst the tunes may be simple, the effect of the constantly overlapping lines can be a complex-sounding contrapuntal texture.

The effect is one of both stillness and motion, and this can be most beautiful and meditative both for listener and singer. The listeners may find the canon particularly enchanting if encircled by the singers.

**"Harmonic Echoes"** is a series of short, canonic chants which can be sung by choirs, small groups of singers or used in vocal workshops and schools. The chants have been successfully trialled, and are now regularly used in a number of Trixi Field's Song Meditation workshops. They are all contemporary, modal canons with themes of Joy, Peace, Light and Stillness running through them.

Although intended for a minimum of 3 voices or groups of voices, they can also be used as solo voice/unison chants if so desired. Accessible, easy to learn and enjoyable to sing, they progress from very simple to more challenging later in the collection.

MP3 tracks of sample performances (unison and canonic), and of backings for each canon are also available for instant download from www.lulu.com/trixifield

# 1. Sing a Song of Life

## Notes on <u>Sing a Song of Life</u>

This simple and quick-to-learn round is marked to accommodate four singers or groups of singers coming in at 2-bar (2-measure) intervals, as illustrated on the Sample Performance recording. It's useful as a choir or singing workshop "warm-up".

For a fuller harmony, this could be sung by eight singers or groups of singers, if the group is large enough. Each group would come in at 1-bar (1-measure) intervals as follows:

*[1] Sing*
*[2] Sing a song*
*[3] Sing a song of*
*[4] life*
*[5] Where there's life there's*
*[6] song*
*[7] Where there's song there's*
*[8] life.*

It's probably a good idea to practice the 4-group version first to ensure a secure performance before trying the 8-group version

# 1. Sing a Song of Life

Music & Lyrics: Trixi Field

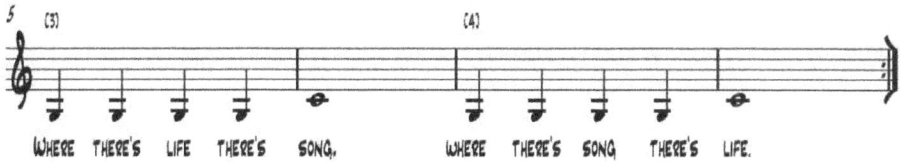

Copyright © 2007

## 2. Be Peace

## Notes on <u>Be Peace</u>

Another very easy round useful as a "warm-up".

Because of its theme and short length, this round has been successfully used as a form of song meditation, both in unison and as a round.

## 2. Be Peace

Music & Lyrics: Trixi Field

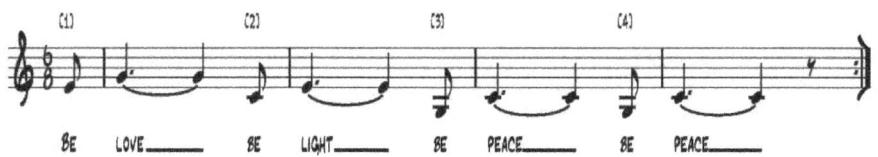

Copyright © 2007

# 3. Dusk Chant

## Notes on <u>Dusk Chant</u>

A good chant to use as a "warm-down" at the end of a voice workshop or rehearsal. This has been a popular chant when trialled in Song Meditation workshops.

Once the full group is confident with the chant, try adding some dynamics: beginning the round *mf*, getting quieter until the word "slumber" is sung *p*.

In previous workshops where the chant has been trialled, the best manageable sound has come from taking breaths as follows:

*As the* √
*sun in the dusk sky* √
*breathes a last sigh* √
*slumber* √

The group could also try lengthening the lines to:

*As the sun in the dusk sky* √
*breathes a last sigh* √
*slumber* √

## 3. Dusk Chant

Music & Lyrics: Trixi Field

Copyright © 2006

# 4. Peace, Sweet and Gentle

## Notes on <u>Peace, Sweet and Gentle</u>

This chant, although still simple, introduces an element which may be a little unfamiliar to our 21st century ears – the Phrygian mode, which has a minor flavour with the addition that the second note in the scale is flattened.

This is excellent for ear training, since the singers will have to listen very carefully to pick up the tune accurately, and try to avoid being influenced by what they *expect* to hear.

It's also a useful breathing exercise. Try singing it with the following breaths:

*Peace, sweet and gentle*√
*Joy fundamental*√
*Joy!*√

And then try the following, but do not despair if the line is too long!

*Peace, sweet and gentle, joy fundamental*√
*Joy!*√

### 4. Peace, Sweet and Gentle

Music & Lyrics: Trixi Field

Copyright © 2006

# 5. My Heart Be Still

## Notes on <u>My Heart Be Still</u>

Also in an ancient mode – the mixolydian mode – it is probably not quite so unfamiliar to our ears, since this mode can be heard quite frequently in popular music. The mixolydian sounds like a major scale, but the 7th note is flattened.

Although the canon is in 6/8, think of it as having a pulse of two beats with triplets on each beat, so that the melody moves strongly and swiftly and doesn't drag.

# 5. My Heart Be Still

Music & Lyrics: Trixi Field

Copyright © 2006

## 6. Still Voices

## Notes on **Still Voices**

In a natural A minor, (or the Aeolian mode), with a descending melodic pattern, juxtaposing sustained notes against gently undulating crotchets (quarter notes). For this chant to work well, singers need to be careful not to split words by taking breaths after each sustained note.

Breaths can be taken as follows:

*Peaceful√*
*strains of√*
*still voices speaking√*
*still hearts seeking√*
*sweet rest√*

It's good to experiment with longer breaths too, perhaps as follows:

*Peaceful strains of√*
*still voices speaking√*
*still hearts seeking√*
*sweet rest√*

Or for the ambitious breathers:

*Peaceful strains of still voices speaking√*
*Still hearts seeking sweet rest√*

# 6. Still Voices

Music & Lyrics: Trixi Field

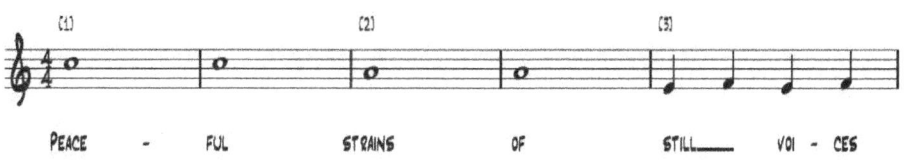

Copyright © 2006

# 7. Dawn Chant

## Notes on Dawn Chant

A two-part piece for two groups of voices, or a group of voices singing the tune, (indicated as voice I on the music) and a group of instruments (strings, woodwind, xylophone – or try any other concert-pitch instrument) playing the second, ostinato part (voice II on the music)

It's a good idea to practise the parts separately first to ensure both groups are secure with their parts. Once they are, try putting the parts together.

Although not initially intended as a canonic chant, trials in workshops - where two groups have sung the tune as a canon and a third group has sung or played the second voice - have worked very well.

If there are enough singers, try splitting the tune into two parts, with the second group coming in after 4 bars (4 measures) as indicated below:

[1] When the sun be-
[2] gins to rise

Once these two groups are confident, try adding the ostinato voice or instrument group.

# 7. Dawn Chant

Music & Lyrics: Trixi Field

Copyright © 2007

## 8. We Are The Song

## Notes on **We Are The Song**

A four-verse canon. This might be best approached by practising verse 1 in unison, then as a canon, and then working similarly through verses 2, 3 and 4.

Once singers are confident with the first verse, the remaining verses should be easy, since the rhythms of their lyrics are similar to those of verse 1.

# 8. We are the Song

Music & Lyrics: Trixi Field

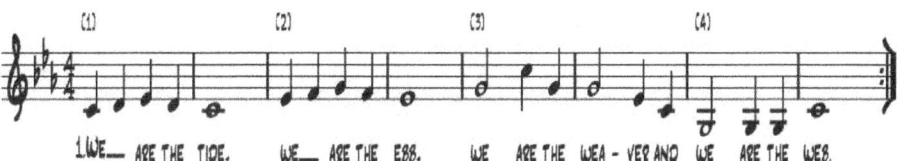

1. We are the tide, we are the ebb, we are the weaver and we are the web.

Verse 2: We are the flow, we are the drift, we are the giver and we are the gift.
Verse 3: We are the words, we are the tune, we are the sun and the stars and the moon.
Verse 4: We are the chime, we are the gong, we are the singer and we are the song.

Copyright © 2007

# 9. Adorian
# (Peace Be In Our Hearts)

## Notes on <u>Adorian (Peace Be In Our Hearts)</u>

In the D Dorian mode but beginning and ending on A, this chant juxtaposes syllabic (one note per syllable) with melismatic melody (two or more notes per syllable). To achieve smoothness, it is best to sing each phrase on one breath.

The final note (on "Peace") is sung only on the final repeat of the chant, to close.

# 9. Adorian

(Peace be in our hearts)

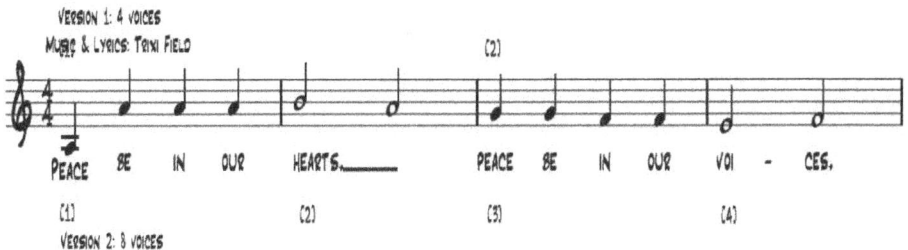

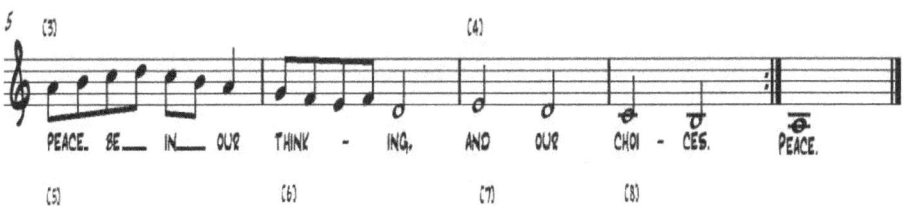

Copyright © 1999, revised 2006

# 10. Light, Soft and Gentle

## Notes on <u>Light, Soft and Gentle</u>

The most challenging chant of the collection, this is in the G Phrygian mode.

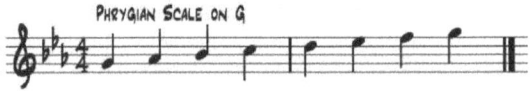

It combines melismatic and syllabic singing in three phrases of 5 bars (5 measures) . Each phrase works best when sung on one breath.

The singers are challenged to listen carefully both to melody, rhythm and length of phrase, and work on steady breathing.

Spend some time working on each individual phrase in unison, perhaps even dividing the phrases into two and three bars (measures) at a time, to break down the learning of the chant into smaller, manageable steps.

Once the group is confident singing the chant in unison, try in two canonic groups, and then in three.

## 10. Light, Soft and Gentle

Music & Lyrics: Trini Field

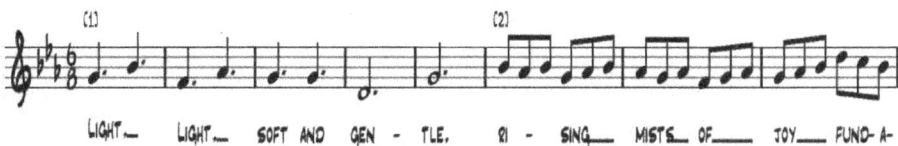

Light— Light— soft and gen - tle, ri - sing mists of— joy— funda-

men - tal. Pil - lars of ev-er-last-ing love mon-u-men - tal

Copyright © 2006

*Lyrics*

# 1. Sing A Song of Life

*Sing!*
*Sing a song*
*Sing a song of life*
*Where there's life there's song!*
*Where there's song there's life!*

Lyrics © 2007 Trixi Field

## 2. Be Peace

*Be love*
*Be light*
*Be peace*
*Be peace*

*Lyrics © 2007 Trixi Field*

## 3. Dusk Chant

*As the sun in the dusk sky*
*Breathes a last sigh*
*Slumber.*

*Lyrics © 2006 Trixi Field*

## 4. Peace, Sweet and Gentle

*Peace*
*Sweet and gentle*
*Joy fundamental*
*Joy*

Lyrics © 2006 Trixi Field

## 5. My Heart Be Still

*My heart, be still*
*And with peace fill*
*Overflowing joy is life's will.*

Lyrics © 2006 Trixi Field

## 6. Still Voices

*Peaceful strains of still voices speaking*
*Still hearts seeking*
*Sweet rest*

Lyrics © 2006 Trixi Field

## 7. Dawn Chant

*When the sun begins to rise*
*Let my heart open with my eyes*

*Lyrics © 2007 Trixi Field*

## 8. We are the song

*Verse 1:*
*we are the tide*
*we are the ebb*
*we are the weaver and we are the web*

*Verse 2:*
*We are the flow*
*We are the drift*
*We are the giver and we are the gift*

*Verse 3:*
*We are the words*
*We are the tune*
*We are the sun and the stars and the moon*

*Verse 4:*
*We are the chime*
*We are the gong*
*We are the singer and we are the song*

Lyrics © 2007 Trixi Field

## 9. Peace Be In Our Hearts

*Peace be in our hearts*
*Peace be in our voices*
*Peace be in our thinking and our choices*
*(Peace).*

Lyrics © 2006 Trixi Field

## 10. Light, Soft and Gentle

*Light, light*
*Soft and gentle*
*Rising mists of joy fundamental*
*Pillars of everlasting love monumental*

Lyrics © 2006 Trixi Field

## *About the composer*

*In our noisy, busy, stressed-out, high-tech society we have, to a large part, become separated from the simple joy of singing and creative music-making – an essential part of being human.*

*Trixi Field's mission is not only to bring joy to others through her own particular styles of music and singing, but to inspire others to find within themselves their own individual voice, to sing with confidence, and to enjoy the delightful togetherness of group singing and music making.*

*To this end, Trixi regularly runs voice workshops and song-meditation workshops in the United Kingdom and abroad. She also composes vocal music for choirs, workshop groups and for schools, jazz songs for soloists and jazz music for bands.*
*She has recorded a handful of her jazz songs on her album "Green", two of which have earned her*

*certificates of honour in the prestigious John Lennon Song Contest in the US.*

*For more information on Trixi's workshops and music you are warmly invited to visit her site at:*
*www.trixifield.co.uk*

*For a full list of her books and compositions currently available, please visit her at:*
*www.lulu.com/trixifield*

www.ingramcontent.com/pod-product-compliance
Lightning Source LLC
Chambersburg PA
CBHW051716040426
42446CB00008B/906